C000155260

DEAR JESUS
WHERE ARE YOU?

DEAR JESUS
WHERE ARE YOU?

EMMAZINA DAY

Copyright © 2021 Emmazina Day.

All rights reserved. No part of this book may be reproduced in any form or by any electronic or mechanical means, including information storage and retrieval systems, without permission in writing from the publisher, except by reviewers, who may quote brief passages in a review.

ISBN: 978-1-63821-038-2 (Paperback Edition)
ISBN: 978-1-63821-039-9 (Hardcover Edition)
ISBN: 978-1-63821-037-5 (E-book Edition)

Some characters and events in this book are fictitious. Any similarity to the real persons, living or dead, is coincidental and not intended by the author.

Book Ordering Information

Phone Number: 315 288-7939 ext. 1000 or 347-901-4920
Email: info@globalsummithouse.com
Global Summit House
www.globalsummithouse.com

Printed in the United State of America

Dedication

I would like to dedicate, this Book to my first Love. My savior Jesus Christ. I give thanks with all of my being without him I am nothing. I would like to thank my family, for their support. For being understanding.

While writing this little book. To my Mother, grandmother who has passed on. Who have always encourage me, by saying, that I can do anything. All I had to do was to put my mind to it. To all my family members who said we love you. Keep writing.

Thank you! Family and friends. For being there at the right time. For me, So many blessing and lessons learned. Sometimes some Friends come and go but God, family and love. Will always Be forever.

Can't Change A Thang!

We cannot go back, in our past. And change anything... But we can certainly start life over. By looking forward, to a new beginning. Starting now. If you wish to, move forward. Keep almighty God, first. in your life, trust and him, Your be happy you did. Believe in the living God. Victory is mine saith the lord he's waiting to hear from you Just sayin"...

Dr. Jesus

What a beautiful name!

What a powerful name Jesus!

What a name we all should know the name is Dr. Jesus! Can anyone think of a time when you needed Jesus. When Jesus, was not there for you. He's always in the midst of all things. I promise you he's there for you. Pray and ask your heavenly father whatever you need from him. Take it all to Jesus…

The bible tells us God die for our sins and he did. So I love to call Jesus name, Jesus sweet Jesus!

The bible tells us Jesus is coming back one day don't know when but he's coming. Just read the book of revelation. Read the bible for yourself it's in there, just saying. Jesus is a jealous God; he loves for us all to pray to him. Call him and the morning call him in the evening there's no charge to ask or talk to Dr. Jesus. Don't turn Jesus away. You do not want your

7

soul to be lost. Jesus can fix every problem and heal every pain. Come on let's bless his name. Im Just saying.

Author Emmazina Day

Hush Your Mouth

We need to be careful of what we say. What you say, can and will be harmful. We need to understand what it means, to say things out of our mouth, that's not cool. Like using profanity. We should not say certain things, because our life is being recorded just like everything else in this world. It's not what I'm saying... it's what the bible tells us. we just need to read and pay attention, and listen to what is the right things to say ...I'm just saying, it's very easy to get caught up and before you know it "Bam!" we have said some slick stuff out of our mouth, it's hard to say the right things, all the time. It's very hard, but like they say nothing comes easy in this world. For most of us. We do have rules to follow, they are called the ten commandments.

The bible says, God said so. Just sayin...
(Matthew 12:36)

Recognize

We need to recognize love, when we see it! love comes in all shapes and sizes. Why wait to let the other person know. How much you really care? Grandmom!

We care we love you, family and friends listen! we all need to show love to one another. Almighty God, blessed us to love and care for each other. When someone we love is helpless or sick . We need to recognize, and not wait until they are no longer with us. Or to say I love you.

But we are quick to say, ok well I'm going to call you but I forgot. I just got so busy working and I just forgot. You may even say I got so busy with the kids. Doing so many things. And I just forgot. I just had no time to visit, there are so many excuses we use. Mother was so tired and I was going to stop by to see you. It's just been one thing or another that's keeping me from visiting. We do not mean any harm, we

all just get caught up, and our own daily lives, so busy we all are. We just forget at times, to take the time, out to say I Love You. To the ones who means, the most to us. We wasn't to busy to say Mother or Grandma, can you, will you take me to the mall or drop me off to the movies whatever the reason is Grandma, Mother or Dad was always there with open arms a loving smile. she or he may say ok come on... let's go... you guys do not make any sense. But guess what Recognize. She took the time out for you! she never said I'm too busy, I just forgot! please stop being so busy, get off the cell phones, get off the computer. Stop. Take a moment and say I Love You! Mom. Would you like to take a walk in the park or just sit and talk. It doesn't cost you anything to call or visit, with a kind word or a hug. Let's say or do something. Your choice but do something memorable, with the one who means something to you. Recognize love when it's right in front of you!

I'M A WARRIOR FOR JESUS

I'm A Warrior For King Jesus

This book is for all ages young and old

When we speak of our Heavenly Father there is no age limit. I'm a Warrior for Dear Jesus is to give guidance to those who may need a little more understanding of what Jesus expects of us.

When we do wonderful things in love, it is of GOD.

When you have faith and belief share your knowledge with others about our heavenly father you then become a warrior for the lord.

The lord said, "well done, good and faithful servant; you were faithful over a few things, I will make you ruler over many things."

(Matthew 25:21)

Four Days...

Did you know that Jesus raised someone from the dead well he did his name is Lazarus! He was the brother of Martha and Mary. Mother heard that Jesus was coming up the road Mary was so upset that her brother had died that she needed to talk and see Jesus, this was during the time Jesus was living on Earth. Doing this time Jesus was going around in the land preaching the word of his father Jehovah God. People in the land heard Jesus was a Healer and then he made the blind man see wow! Willy bellie kids (it is all in there) where you might at the Bible you see kids you must have faith you must believe Jesus died for you and for me! when Jesus saw Mary, her neighbors and they were so upset that Lazarus had died! what do you think happened? Jesus was upset was upset too. And he wept. Meaning he cried) the neighbor said Jesus loved him so very much Mary got on her knees she said Jesus if you have been here my brother, would *have not died. My brother has been dead for four days, Mary was so heartbroken tears rolling down her cheeks take me to where my brother Lazarus is, Mary her sister Martha, took Jesus to a cave with a big round stone for a door is where Lazarus was. He was in a deep sleep. The stone was removed from the cave Jesus looked up into the sky and started to pray. Wellie kids if you look up at the sky that's where Heaven is. Way beyond the stars in the moon how do we know you may ask? because when Jesus was praying for Lazarus Jesus lifted up his eyes to heaven and started to pray father I thank you for hearing my prayer and for answering my prayer. I know you hear me always. Your neighbor that's standing by will believe, that you sent me. When Jesus stop praying he shouted Lazarus come out! he came out of the cave wrap and white cloth and the cloth was covering his whole body Jesus asked the people to help Lazarus and he was able go home with his family. I'm sure Lazarus was happy to see his family once again I know Mary and Martha all of the neighbors said thank you Jesus! Everyone was happy full of faith and believe this was truly a blessing from Heaven. Willy Bellie kids keep praying keep the faith Jesus remember God is what? always listening.*

LOVE

My Love, I'm attracted to you. your qualities that you display, I love you for all your abilities you possess. God has given you so many blessings, To love Another My love. I love the way you smell, the way you touch and lift my hand towards your lips and kiss my hand. Indeed without saying the respect that comes with loving one Another makes my heart have two beats of love that sings a song just for. US.

God has given us love for each other.

The Lord is my light and my salvation whom shall I fear? The Lord is the stronghold of my life - of whom shall I be afraid? I will have faith belief. And love my savior Jesus Christ; he died for me and you Welly Bellie Kids.

Psalm 27:1

Messages Of Love
Dear Jesus

★ *Love is God*

★ *Love is respect for each other*

★ *Love is being in love*

★ *Love is tears of joy*

★ *Love is so deep it never dies*

★ *Love is so powerful*

★ *Love is true*

★ *Love is so real*

★ *Love is peace*

★ *Love is forever*

★ *Love is family*

★ *Love is a feeling*

★ *Love is a gift from heaven*

Love has no words to explain

Love is Dear Jesus he died for you and I.

My Prayer

I come to you

In prayer, Dear Jesus, I'm expressing my love to you. For allowing me to live and raise my family. Also for being a Mother, wife, sister and grandmother. What a blessing Father, that you have allowed me to be a great-aunt. Also a loving friend. Thank you Father, for loving me. And giving me the strength to be able to help others. Father, please bring peace and guidance to us all. So that we can continue to move forward in life. What a blessing it has been for me to grow in faith. To gain knowledge to learn from my challenges. I say thank you! Father, I ask of you, could you please continue to, bless my family and friends, with good health. Please keep us safe from harm's way. I'm so thankful Dear Jesus for your grace and your mercy. For showing us how to be humble I will forever love you Amen.

Mother and Daughter's Love

A Mother's love for her daughter. Is a love, you cannot describe. When a mother loves you, she loves you unconditionally, she's there for your every whim, every tear that falls You can count on your mother. To be there for her daughter. A daughter loves her Mother with so much love, she respects her and she' proud to be her daughter.

Mother is there to talk to her daughter, when she's older. And she really needs Mother, Daughter realize Mother can wipe away her tears, from her cheeks. Put a loving smile on her face.

Mother will take all her worries and frustrations, away by sitting you down for a nice home cooked meal made just the way you like it. A glass of your favorite beverage and feel your heart up with

wisdom, the tone of her voice will ease the tear you have shared with Mom. Mother, will Listen to you with whatever you have on your mind. Will then look at you and say everything will be alright my daughter, with a smile only a mother can give, you hear her voice and you just know you're ok. Mother is always called Mom. Or mommy, There are known words to say, because Mom's will say whatever she feels her heart needs to say to her child whether it's right or wrong we listen to Mom. We do not follow her advice, at times. We grow weak, when we stray away. Sometimes we do not listen to Mom, when she speaks knowledge into our hearts. Are we listening? Sometimes, we are and sometimes not. Some of us daughters act like we have all the answers and we do not. Not realizing how much of this knowledge she's trying to relay to us, is very important to our hearts and mind. Until you're much older. Then we realize, Jesus says. honor your mother and your Father and your days shall be long upon the land.

A mother is a strong woman whose love has no ending for her children. No matter what age, they may become. Mother can feed you, like she feeds her baby, Without having a bottle. Or having to wash

a bottle. As you get older, she will still feed you with advice. She will never sugar coat the truth this is the way God has made a woman. A woman with soft skin and soft hands. When she looks into your eyes. She means what she says. And she says what she means Almighty God, knew exactly what he was doing, when he made a woman, called Mother. One thing we know we cannot live on this earth, without a woman called Mother Cherish your Mom always.

ABOUT THE AUTHOR

Emmazina Day lives in Virginia, she has a passion to write short stories, Ms. Day would like to share with anyone who has love for Jesus. Ms. Day is dedicating this book to her family and all of the Wellie Bellie kids…Ms. Day says… I would like to believe Jesus, is in the wind there´s a warm breeze you cannot see him only feel the warmth of the cool embrace of the invisible wind you can only feel, our heavenly father. He is always with you and me.

Lightning Source UK Ltd.
Milton Keynes UK
UKHW050500270521
384314UK00008B/54